Creating Value
Through eCommerce

Financial Times Management Briefings are happy to receive proposals from individuals who have expertise in the field of management education.

If you would like to discuss your ideas further, please contact Andrew Mould, Commissioning Editor.

Tel: 0171 447 2210
Fax: 0171 240 5771
e-mail: andrew.mould@ftmanagement.com

MANAGEMENT BRIEFINGS

GENERAL MANAGEMENT

Creating Value Through eCommerce

JOHN O'CONNOR AND EAMONN GALVIN

FINANCIAL TIMES
MANAGEMENT

FINANCIAL TIMES

MANAGEMENT

LONDON · SAN FRANCISCO
KUALA LUMPUR · JOHANNESBURG

Financial Times Management delivers the knowledge,
skills and understanding that enable students,
managers and organisations to achieve their ambitions,
whatever their needs, wherever they are.

London Office:
128 Long Acre, London WC2E 9AN
Tel: +44 (0)171 447 2000
Fax: +44 (0)171 240 5771
Website: www.ftmanagement.com

A Division of Financial Times Professional Limited

First published in Great Britain 1998

© Financial Times Professional Limited 1998

The right of John O'Connor and Eamonn Galvin to be identified as authors
of this work has been asserted by them in accordance
with the Copyright, Designs, and Patents Act 1988.

ISBN 0 273 63581 6

British Library Cataloguing in Publication Data
A CIP catalogue record for this book can be obtained from the British Library.

10 9 8 7 6 5 4 3 2 1

Typeset by Boyd Elliott Typesetting
Printed and bound in Great Britain

The Publishers' policy is to use paper manufactured from sustainable forests.

About the authors

John O'Connor is an Associate Partner with Andersen Consulting. He has consulted to a wide range of blue-chip organisations across Europe for more than ten years, including Aer Lingus, AIB Bank, Barclays Bank, British Gas, Esso, Hewlett-Packard, Microsoft, NatWest, SAS Airlines and TSB Bank.

Eamonn Galvin is a specialist in strategy consulting with Andersen Consulting. He has lectured widely in marketing and has consulted to a wide range of clients including Aer Lingus, Associated British Foods, Guinness, Kwik Save, Transco, Microsoft and Waterford Foods.

John and Eamonn write and lecture regularly on the subject of eCommerce. They are the authors of *Marketing and Information Technology*, published by Pitman Publishing in 1997.

They can be contacted by e-mail at:

john.r.oconnor@ac.com

eamonn.galvin@ac.com

Contents

Executive summary

Electronic commerce, or eCommerce, receives considerable attention at senior management levels. Dramatic success stories in industries as diverse as bookselling (Amazon.com), computer equipment (Dell Computers) and engineering (General Electric) are held up as shining examples of how eCommerce can generate real wealth.

The purpose of this briefing is to provide a pragmatic assessment of the eCommerce market and enable senior executives to make decisions about whether or not it is appropriate for their businesses. This is an important point. For some, it may not be appropriate. At least not yet.

Many of the success stories we discuss, hail from the US. Certainly, North America is the most developed eCommerce market in the world and is likely to remain so for some years to come. For this reason alone, senior executives would be well advised to buy a plane ticket to New York, Chicago or San Francisco, visit with their counterparts and learn from their experiences (both good and bad).

Good and bad, because for every success story, there are hundreds of expensive eCommerce failures. The majority of failures are characterised by an inability to understand what really drives eCommerce and what it takes to become a player in the eCommerce game.

In the course of this management briefing, we will seek to answer three fundamental questions:

- What is driving the explosive growth of eCommerce?
- How can businesses create value using eCommerce?
- How do you implement an eCommerce solution?

What is driving the explosive growth of eCommerce?

While the eCommerce market is very new there are a number of drivers which should continue to see the market expand.

- **Customers are embracing eCommerce.** At the heart of the growth of eCommerce is the rapid penetration of Internet access at a consumer level. Currently over 60 million customers worldwide have access to eCommerce through the Internet and this is set to continue growing. Consumers are already purchasing goods and services over the Internet and, more importantly for UK and European businesses, the business-to-consumer eCommerce market is finally taking off outside the US.

- **Businesses are achieving real benefits from eCommerce.** Current indicators are that the business-to-business market is already a major market and likely to continue to grow even faster than its consumer counterpart. Moreover, businesses are already achieving real benefits from business-to-business eCommerce.

- **The supporting infrastructure is finally being put in place.** Organisations and consumers are investing heavily in the basic technology infrastructure required for eCommerce such as high capacity telecommunications networks and more powerful PCs. Companies such as Sony are also developing innovative new ways of accessing the Internet through television. New payment mechanisms are being developed and, although one of the major constraints on growth is the issue of Internet security, this is being addressed by the rapid development of encryption software. Also, the development of other industries such as overnight package delivery makes it feasible to deliver products directly to customers without investing heavily in a distribution network.

How can businesses create value using eCommerce?

Capitalising on eCommerce opportunities requires senior managers to:

- **Understand how eCommerce creates value.** The concept of eCommerce changes the way companies create value. It puts more power in the hands of customers by making product and price information from different suppliers easier

to access and compare. It can also reduce the cost of doing business by eliminating or shortening process cycles. In general, eCommerce can affect industries in different ways:

- it can create a variety of new technology-based products and services;

- it can create new and more efficient markets, particularly in areas such as catalogue sales, brand name goods and information-intensive or digital goods;

- it can enable new business processes which can help organisations to cut costs, reduce lead times and slash inventory levels.

- **Decide the level of eCommerce at which to operate.** There are typically four levels that companies go through in their development of eCommerce.

  - **publish** – the first level whereby companies provide a one-way flow of information to customers through a Web page or Web site;

  - **interact** – the second level whereby the flow of information becomes two-way and companies begin to develop a relationship with their customers;

  - **transact** – the third level whereby buyers and sellers of products and services can trade on-line;

  - **integrate** – the final level whereby full business partnerships are created between organisations that integrate their core business processes.

As companies progress from one level to the next, the interaction with the customer increases and so does the level of investment. Typically the largest benefits occur at the higher levels but changes to existing business processes are necessary at every level.

How do you implement an eCommerce solution?

In order to implement a successful eCommerce solution, senior managers must:

- **Start by building a sound business case.** This should include the impact that eCommerce will have on the business in the areas of investment, sales and operating costs. Although increased reach and additional sales are usually the primary reasons for taking companies on-line, the business case can also be built around cost reduction in areas such as procurement. Business cases will differ

greatly from industry to industry but the most important message for senior
executives is that many of the serious eCommerce players are making major
investments and buying market share at the expense of short-term profits. In
other words, the business case is based on strategic long-term positioning rather
than attractive ROI figures and short payback periods.

- Apply the guiding principles for successful eCommerce. Senior executives need to
  bear the following principles in mind as they embark on an eCommerce initiative:

  - Always start with the customer proposition.

  - Think creatively about how to design your key processes.

  - Commit your best executives.

  - Create 'value networks' to attract customers.

  - Apply leverage to your customers and suppliers.

  - 'Think big, start small and scale quickly.'

- **Make a start.** If the fundamentals are right for your business there is no time like
  the present. Early movers are already carving out profitable markets. If you are
  ready to make a start, there are four relatively straightforward steps to follow:

  - **Step 1:** Conduct an honest self-evaluation of your capabilities.

  - **Step 2:** Decide if there is a business case for change.

  - **Step 3:** Gear up for implementation.

  - **Step 4:** Just do it!

Part 1

WHAT IS DRIVING THE EXPLOSIVE GROWTH OF eCOMMERCE?

1

What is eCommerce?

A definition of eCommerce

The term electronic commerce, or eCommerce for short, can be used to describe any trading activity that is carried out over an electronic network such as the Internet. Nowadays, many people assume that the Internet or the World Wide Web is the electronic network when the term eCommerce is mentioned. However, electronic commerce was being conducted long before the Internet or World Wide Web were invented. For decades, banks have been conducting and settling business electronically worth trillions of pounds every day. In France, the Minitel system has served millions of consumers and businesses for almost as long. The French mail order company La Redoute gets 20 per cent of its orders by Minitel and the French rail system handles 24 million transactions a year through the same medium. However, for this briefing we have focused mainly on eCommerce conducted through the Internet. We have also taken a broader definition of eCommerce than some other commentators might, by including activities which do not always result in a financial transaction taking place, such as customer requests for product information. As we will see later, there is a broad spectrum of eCommerce activity ranging from the provision of information through to the sale of products and services involving financial transactions. Given the central role of the Internet in eCommerce, it is useful at this point to look at its development.

A short history of the Internet and the World Wide Web

The Internet is a collection of interrelated computer access and information and networks which span the globe and allow users with PCs and the right software to communicate with each other. Conceived as a US government research project in 1969, it was not until 1993 that public interest in the Internet really took off. When a newer, mult media version of the Internet was invented, known as the World Wide Web. The World Wide Web (WWW, or Web for short) has allowed companies and individuals to add colour, graphics, video and other multimedia capabilities to the messages that they leave on the Internet. The scale of the improvement can be likened to moving from black and white silent movies straight into full colour with surround sound. The recent growth of the Intenet has been little short of phenomenal

and it has evolved from being primarily a messaging service to a medium for advertising, marketing and selling products and services.

As well as its user-friendliness, there are a number of other benefits which help explain the rapid growth of the Internet and eCommerce:

- Access is open to all users who have access to a PC, a phone line and the correct software.

- It is accessible to people with limited technical knowledge.

- The low cost of setting up a Web site has reduced barriers to entry, although as we shall see later, the cost of setting up the Web site is probably one of the lowest of the overall costs.

Understanding the likely impact of eCommerce

The creation of the Web in 1993 provided a major boost for eCommerce which has since seen an enormous influx of capital and creativity. However, while it is still in the early stages of development, there are three basic characteristics of eCommerce which make it imperative that senior executives understand the likely impact it will have on their businesses:

- **It is pervasive.** It may have started life as a US phenomenon but it now transcends geographic, cultural, industry and political boundaries.

- **It creates new, rich sources of value.** For some organisations, the attraction to eCommerce is its potential to reduce costs, but the ultimate value of eCommerce is that it creates new products and services, new markets and new ways to build relationships with customers.

- **It changes the rules.** eCommerce changes the way an organisation must think about its physical and organisational structures; it creates new sources of competition; and it blurs the lines that separate industries.

Currently, eCommerce is a grand mixture of both hype and substance. However, when all is said and done, eCommerce will have a major impact on businesses because the drivers are sound and the market is set for continued rapid growth. The three key drivers behind this growth are:

- consumers are embracing eCommerce;

- businesses are achieving real benefits from eCommerce;

- the supporting infrastructure for eCommerce is finally being put in place.

We shall now look at each of these key drivers in more detail.

2

Consumers are embracing eCommerce

The key driver for any new industry is strong consumer demand. In eCommerce there are a number of very positive demand trends:

- the number of Internet users continues to rise;

- users are buying more and more goods over the Internet;

- the market outside the US is finally taking off.

The number of Internet users continues to rise

By 2002, over 50 per cent of US households are expected to be on-line. In Europe the estimate is 25 per cent; in Asia-Pacific, it is 15 per cent. The number of people on-line in the US is expected to increase from 37 million in 1996 to 116 million in 2002, which will represent over 40 per cent of the US population (*see* Figure 2.1). The compound annual growth rate (CAGR) is over 20 per cent a year. These estimates are convincing commercial organisations that there is a massive latent demand for on-line goods and services.

Figure 2.1
Growth in people and households on-line 1996–2002

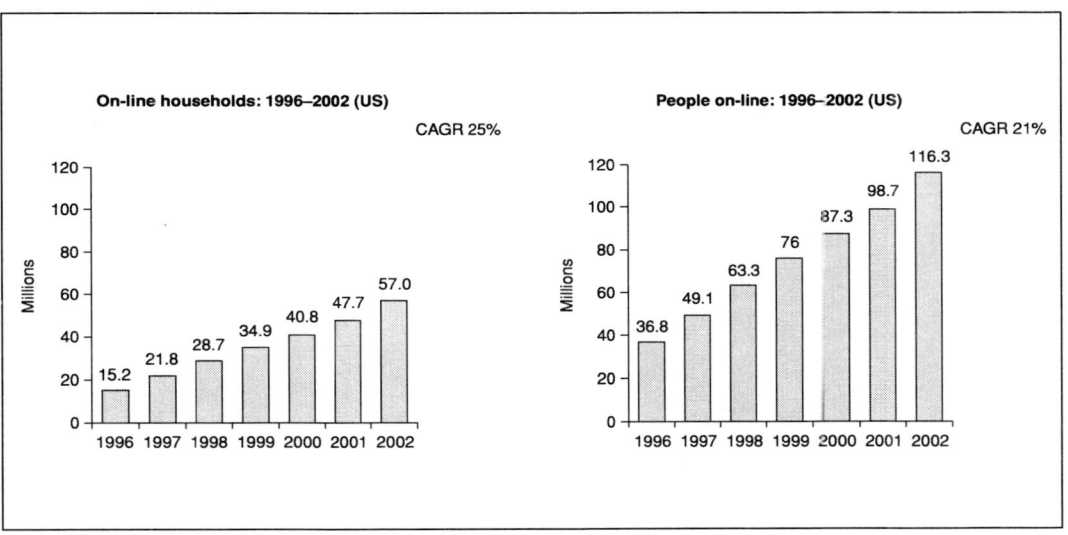

Source: Jupiter Communications 1998 Online Shopping Report.

It is important to understand what is driving this rapid rate of growth. While many users were initially curious about the Internet, that does not explain why so many people are embracing it. The truth is that the Internet adds value in a number of ways. Initially customers enjoy the ability to search and retrieve information on any particular topic. The WWW is better than the largest encyclopaedia as it is updating

knowledge in real time. For example, a search on an obscure topic such as Go, the Japanese version of chess, provides access to existing documentation on the game. It also provides access to other users who are interested in the game and people can participate in newsgroups where more detailed discussions on the finer points of the game are debated. If you are really interested in the game you will also find books advertised for sale and even tutors for hire. This progression from seeking out information, communicating with others and finally transacting some kind of trade is a theme which runs throughout eCommerce.

Users are buying more and more goods over the Internet

In 1995, goods and services sold to consumers via the Internet totalled $70 million worldwide. By 1996 the total had increased to over $500 million. Market watchers continue to revise eCommerce projections upwards and US consumer spending is now forecasted to exceed $40 billion and worldwide spending to exceed $90 billion by 2002. The estimates from two separate eCommerce-watchers in Figure 2.2 illustrate how on-line sales are growing faster than originally expected.

Figure 2.2
Changes in projected growth in eCommerce sales

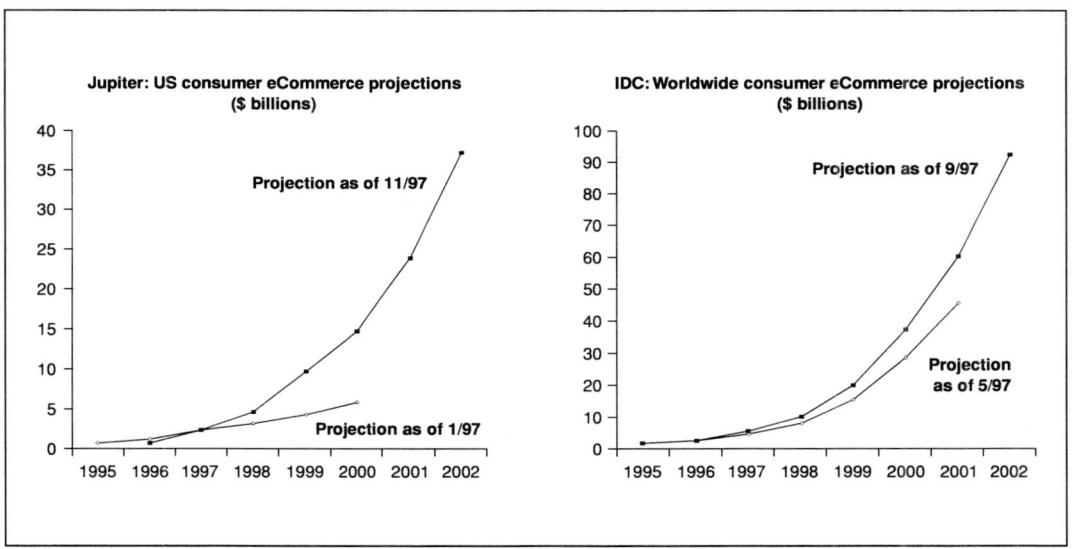

Regardless of which study you believe, Internet commerce will clearly represent a significant opportunity for those businesses that can effectively capitalise on it. One

measure of which areas are growing the fastest is 'reach'. Reach is defined as the number of unique individuals who visit a specific site as a percentage of the total number of users who access the Internet that month. Reach can be defined for industries or individual sites. Consumers currently visit software, books and gift sites most often but music sites are expected to achieve the greatest reach in the future. However, the projected revenues to be achieved through on-line sales tell a different story – the average size of travel, hardware and grocery transactions will make these the largest online consumer markets in the future.

'Reach' for selected industries (1997 and 2002) is shown in Figure 2.3, while the estimated revenue to be gained is shown in Figure 2.4.

Figure 2.3
Projected 'reach' for selected industries 1997–2002

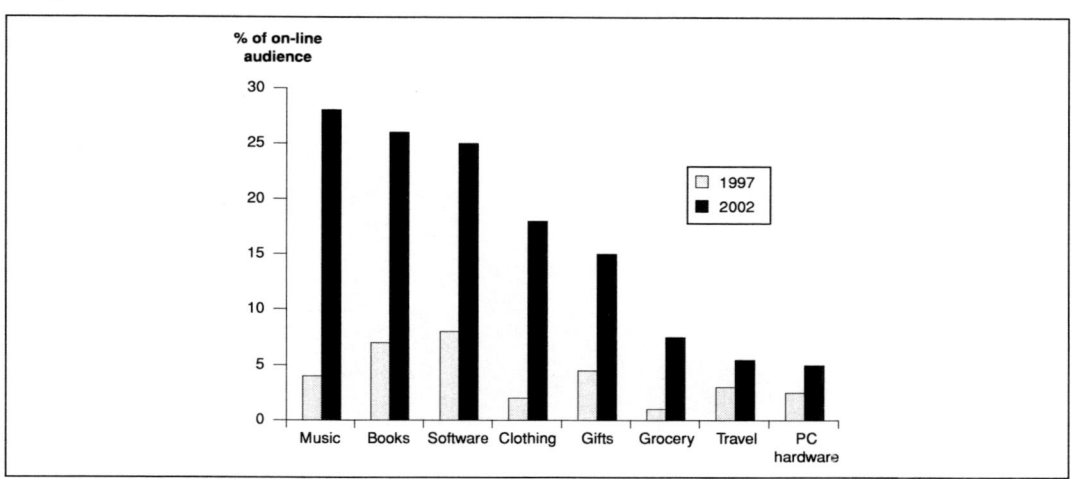

Figure 2.4
Projected revenue for selected industries 1997–2002

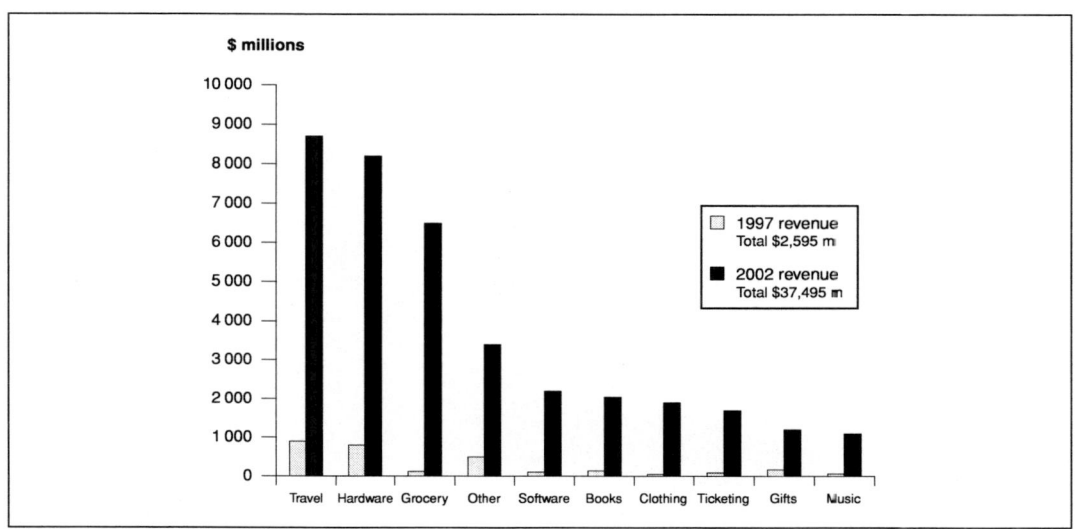

> **INSIGHT**: Cisco, the manufacturer of network products, uses its 'Cisco Connection' (http://www.cisco.com) Web site to handle sales. Currently almost 40 per cent of its $4 billion plus turnover is processed in this new channel which is also used to build stronger relationships with its customers. Over 500 000 customers a month access their Web site to download software and log technical queries. Each customer's transaction is recorded to build up a profile and identify opportunities to improve service. The bonus for Cisco is that, while it is making it easy for customers to do business, it is also saving operating expenses estimated at $270 million a year.

So what is the attraction for on-line customers? Broadly speaking, there are three main benefits:

- **Price.** Customers expect to pay less for goods purchased electronically, on the assumption that businesses will reduce sales and distribution costs and pass savings to the end customer. Customers can browse through lists of products, and compare prices against the competition.

- **Convenience.** Buyers can purchase a wide range of products anytime and anywhere, from the comfort of their own home or office.

- **Individualised service.** Buyers can design their own products and services, and make specific requests for products which suit their own tastes and preferences.

> **MANAGEMENT TIP:** Don't assume that 'if you build it, they will come' strategies work.
>
> Companies that relied primarily on the 'if you build it, they will come' strategy typically found little success in these early ventures. For example, MarketPlaceMCI, MCI's electronic shopping mall, was introduced in April 1995, and closed its doors a little over a year later. According to an MCI executive, the mall failed in part because catalogue vendors didn't put their full inventories on-line and insisted on lots of flashy graphics which were difficult to download. MCI is not alone in its rush to employ eCommerce within the consumer market. Other companies like AT&T, Nets Inc., and the Vermont Teddy Bear Co. also jumped in and have since closed their Internet doors. But more of this later.

The market outside of the US is finally taking off

Until very recently, the business-to-consumer eCommerce market was primarily confined to the US. While the US will continue to be the largest and most well-developed market for many years to come, other countries are starting to catch up. Indeed, there are opportunities for emerging economies to leap-frog traditional stages of market development and, in the process, potentially surpass other regions not only in infrastructure but also in competitive ability.

When looking at the potential for growth in non-US markets there are two key drivers which will determine how quickly markets will reach critical mass:

- **The number of people with access to the infrastructure.** The number of telephones and computers required for eCommerce (preferably through digital lines) must be large enough to constitute a marketplace and, on this measure, the US is likely to continue to be the main market.

- **Average spending power.** Based on gross domestic product and savings rates, this must be high enough to offset the cost of product development, marketing and delivery.

All the indications are that most Northern European countries, including the UK, are likely to experience major growth in the coming years. In addition, some of the larger economies in Asia-Pacific are likely to see a major increase in Internet commerce (*see* Figure 2.5).

Figure 2.5
Key drivers of market development

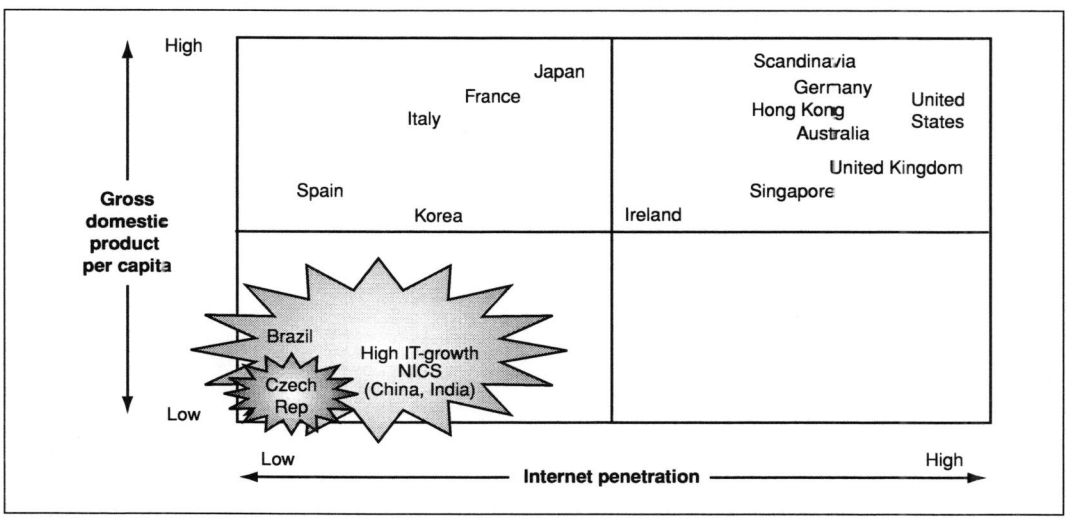

CASE STUDY 2.1: Wal-Mart increases its customer base

Wal-Mart

Wal-Mart is a leading retailer in the US that is continuously seeking to enlarge its customer base. One means of achieving this goal is to seek out customers living far from existing Wal-Mart stores as well as those consumers who are willing to pay for convenience. Wal-Mart has developed a 'one-stop shopping' experience by partnering with other retailers to provide a wider range of services and selling fresh foods such as seafood. Their on-line offering has 27 merchandise categories with more than 140 000 items, which is double the number of stock-keeping units (SKUs) that can be displayed in physical stores. Wal-Mart has positioned its on-line offering as a 'convenient, time-saving shopping alternative to customers that makes their lives easier'.

Results

- On-line sales contributed $20 million to overall revenues of approximately $120 billion in 1997 and are expected to grow rapidly.

- 'Reach' increased 17 per cent in six months to 0.7 per cent in February 1998.

- Best-selling items include products like Rolex watches and Nike T-shirts which are not sold in physical stores.

- US military personnel stationed overseas have been one of the most enthusiastic customer segments.

3

Businesses are achieving real benefits from eCommerce

While the business-to-consumer eCommerce market is growing, the business-to-business market has been expanding even more quickly. To a large extent, this market was already established in the form of electronic data interchange (EDI) long before the label 'eCommerce' appeared. EDI refers to the linking of trading partners across a common network and is usually associated with the automation of elements of the 'billing cycle' such as automated transmission of invoices and purchase orders between trading partners. The difference is that EDI, while cost-effective, tends to be difficult to implement and restricted to small collectives of trading partners that agree to adopt common standards and practices, usually dictated by the biggest player in a supply chain. By contrast, eCommerce is more flexible, more interactive and, in theory, open to any enterprise on the network, large or small, that wants to participate.

There are a number of key trends in the business-to-business market:

- business-to-business eCommerce is already a major market;
- further significant growth is also predicted;
- companies are achieving real benefits from business-to-business eCommerce.

Business-to-business eCommerce is already a major market

The business-to-business market is already a much bigger eCommerce market than its business-to-consumer counterpart. Yet it is the consumer market that receives the greatest coverage and exposure. While consumers were purchasing in excess of $1 billion per annum over the Internet by the end of 1997, General Electric alone purchases over $1 billion of goods from its suppliers each year over the Internet, and most of Dell Computer's Internet sales (also worth approximately $1 billion a year) are to business, rather than personal, customers.

What is more, this trend is unlikely to change. Most industry commentators predict that about 70 per cent of the future eCommerce market will be of the business-to-business variety.

Further significant growth is predicted

Latest projections place the total value of business-to-business eCommerce transactions worldwide somewhere between $62 billion and $160 billion by the year 2000 (*see* Figure 3.1). Although the range of the estimates is significant, there is no doubt that this market is potentially huge.

Figure 3.1

Worldwide projected growth of business-to-business eCommerce

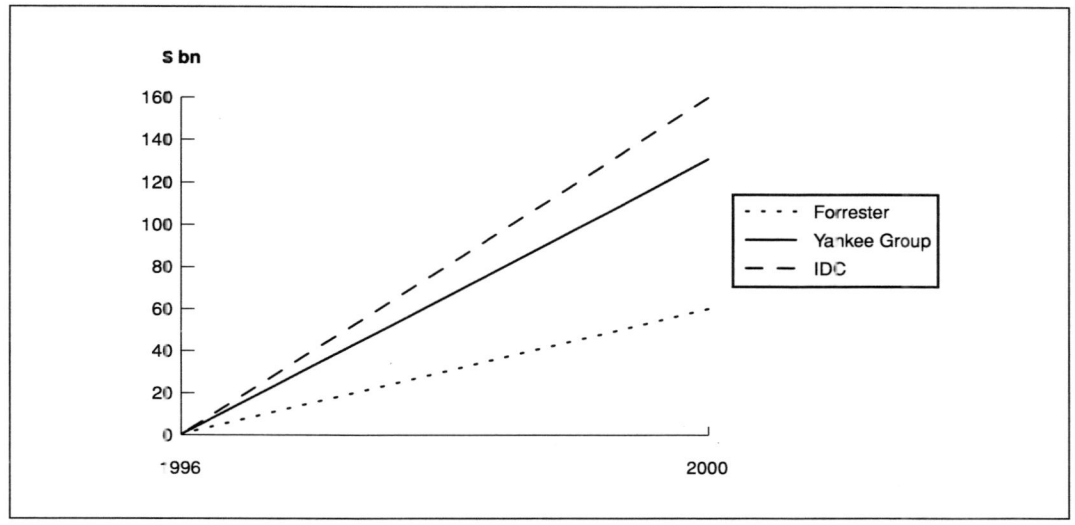

Source: CommerceNet & Nielsen Media Research, Internet Demographics survey, March 1996 and August 1995.

Companies are achieving real benefits from business-to-business eCommerce

Although the potential for business-to-consumer eCommerce is huge, very few returns have yet to be achieved by its major proponents. Contrast this with business-to-business eCommerce where significant benefits have already been realised (*see* Figure 3.2). Purchasing is a good example of an area where companies have used the Internet to establish closer relationships with their customers and suppliers, and have managed to drive down costs significantly in the process.

Figure 3.2

Percent of respondents using the WWW for purchasing

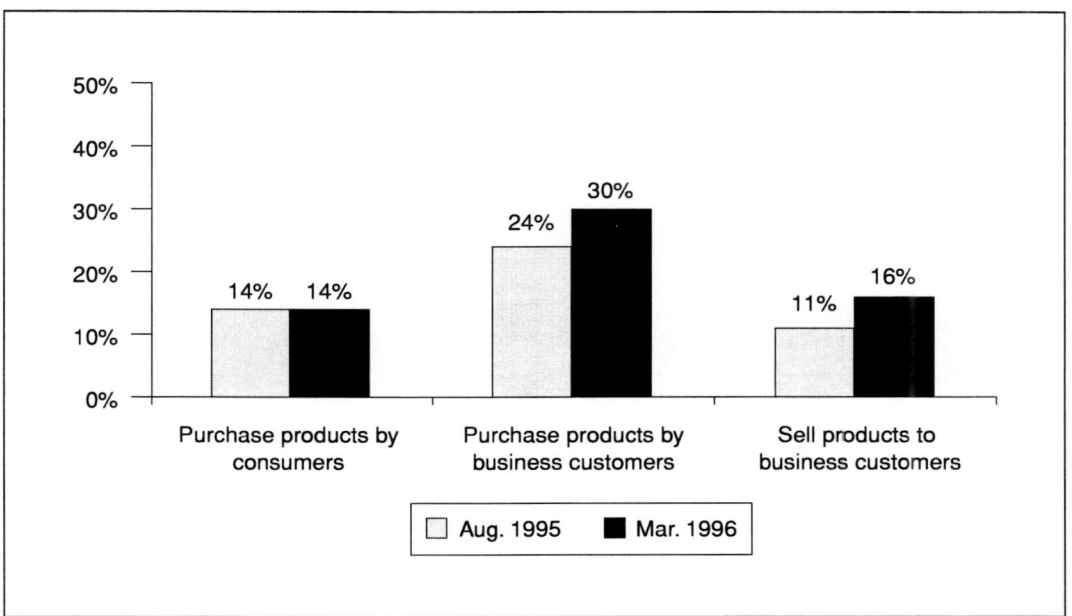

Cost reductions are also being achieved in a number of other ways. High cost channels such as expensive sales forces have been eliminated and savings have been achieved through the automation of existing manual processes where, for example, business customers are given Internet access to information on product availability without the need to go through a human operator. The creation of closer relationships between manufacturer and supplier has provided the impetus for more single-sourcing of goods, with accompanying reductions in prices for bulk orders.

The global nature of the Internet is also giving organisations access to a much broader audience of business customers. For small specialist suppliers with limited resources, the Internet provides them with an opportunity to grow without having to establish dealer networks in other countries. Companies can also develop deeper relationships with their business customers through dialogue and service agreements. Accessing customers directly can also reduce channel costs although, as we will see later, this has to be managed carefully.

CASE STUDY 3.1: General Electric reduces procurement costs

General Electric

General Electric is one of the world's foremost engineering services companies. Through its GE Information Services division, General Electric manages a trading community of several thousand companies through a system known as the Trading Process Network (TPN).

Trading Process Network (TPN)

TPN helps several of GE's own business units, as well as other third parties, to locate new suppliers worldwide, streamline purchasing processes and shorten cycle times. TPN also assists sellers in shortening sales processes and reducing sales costs by automating sales, bidding and ordering. The TPN system is aimed at buyers and suppliers in the industrial manufacturing, automotive and aerospace industries.

One of the TPN systems, TPNPost, enables buyers to manage the procurement process by helping them to identify suppliers, distribute requests for quotations (RFQs) and specifications, transmit electronic drawings to multiple suppliers, hold multiple bidding rounds, and receive and manage bids. The lower costs of processing a bid allows GE to send out more RFQs to suppliers which results in lower procurement costs.

TPN's strengths are its captive supplier base and branded cataloguing method and already over $1 bn worth of goods are procured through the system. The stated objective of General Electric is to migrate all of its centralised purchasing to TPN by the year 2000.

Results

To date, results have been impressive:

- GE has shaved $500 million – $700 million (~ 30 per cent) off its purchasing costs over three years;
- manual processing systems have been automated and cycle times have been reduced, in some cases by up to 50 per cent;

- actual materials costs have been reduced by between 5 and 20 per cent, depending on the item that is sourced;

- 60 per cent of procurement staff have been redeployed and sourcing staff have an additional six days a month to focus on strategic activities.

Lessons learned

While TPN has been largely successful GE learned some painful lessons:

- **Pricing issues** – GE found considerable resistance to the per-transaction pricing it attempted to implement. In any business negotiations, both supplier and buyer need to feel that the basis for doing business is fair and equitable.

- **People issues** – Persuading and co-ordinating GE's own business units to move to TPN also proved more difficult than originally anticipated.

- **Technical issues** – bringing a large number of trading partners on-line can take considerable effort and requires significant understanding of the technical and process issues involved.

- **Telecommunications issues** – building the right international telecommunications infrastructure to support TPN was not always easy. One oft-quoted example of GE Lighting's success in finding Hungarian suppliers that were considerably cheaper fails to mention the telecommunications difficulties that had to be overcome to make the venture work.

4

The supporting infrastructure is finally being put in place

Although technology is not a subject which endears itself to many senior executives, there are certain key facts about Internet technology and other supporting infrastructure which do need to be understood at senior levels:

- access to the Internet is becoming more pervasive;

- the communications infrastructure is evolving;

- business applications for processing transactions are improving;

- growth in other service industries is facilitating eCommerce;

- security is a major issue but steps are being taken to address it.

Access to the Internet is becoming more pervasive

The growth of the World Wide Web was a result of the development of a friendly PC interface, known as a 'browser', which made it easy to navigate the Internet. The importance of this user-friendliness will continue to be a determinant of future growth as Web designers continue to build innovative screens which attract users' attention. For example, the Whitbread Web site which provided coverage of the recent Round The World Race had a very attractive interface which included daily video updates from the sailors participating in the event. Bringing interviews plus the sounds and excitement of the race to life on a PC screen was one of the reasons for the site's huge popularity and very high daily 'hit' rate (number of visitors per day).

From a commercial perspective, the importance of the layout and attractiveness of a Web page is similar to the physical layout of a store front. Good Web site designs can help in developing sales, but they also need to be supported by a good product offering. While a well-located store front on a busy street will always attract passing customers, the same cannot be said of the Internet. Consumers do not simply visit your site. They have to be attracted in. As we will see in Chapter 8, there are several mechanisms that can be employed to achieve this, including the creation of 'on-line communities'.

More important than any of the above points are the recent developments in television technology. Companies like Sony are developing alternative delivery

channels whereby consumers can access the Internet through their existing television screens. Many commentators believe that the full potential of the Internet will never be realised until the Web can be brought into the living room and onto the television screen rather than through a PC. That day is not far off – the technology to support it already exists.

The communications infrastructure is evolving

One of the more powerful recent catchphrases was US Vice-President Gore's description of the 'Information Superhighway'. In the information age, the telecommunications network is the highway upon which the electronic traffic must pass. Unfortunately, until recently it has simply not been wide enough to cater for the vast amounts of traffic that are generated by eCommerce. The capacity, or 'bandwidth', of the standard telephone network is simply not up to the job.

From the perspective of the consumer, this is an important point because bandwidth means speed. In fact, one of the most revealing demonstrations that can be given to any board member who is not familiar with the Internet is a display of how slow the Internet actually is when downloading information from the World Wide Web. Web pages which are very graphical contain considerably more data than simple text-based ones. However, the telecommunications infrastructure is being expanded and improved all the time. Eventually, speed and bandwidth will not be a major inhibitor to business-to-consumer eCommerce. Digital exchanges, fibre-optic networks and other high-speed transmission technologies will increase the speed of Internet communications and further stimulate the eCommerce market.

Business applications for processing transactions are improving

Once an organisation with an eCommerce site starts to receive communications from customers in the form of requests for information or orders it must process these requests. If it has to rely on manual intervention it has no difference in cost structure from another delivery channel such as a call centre. The real cost savings come from being able to automate these processes so that transactions are dealt

with automatically. The growth of eCommerce has led to considerable investment in software which will do just that. An example is the SAP software application which is used to integrate all aspects of an organisation's business from finance to manufacturing. It is one of the fastest growing software packages in the world and can now interface into the Internet to process transactions. Many other popular software applications are also building interfaces to the Internet.

Other important applications which are also being developed include:

- **Secure payment systems** which will allow customers to transact with companies without worrying about security. These can encrypt data to protect it and erect 'firewalls' which protect organisations from unwanted hackers and viruses.

- **Adaptive response applications** which can analyse a customer database and send particular types of data to certain customers based on their personal profiles. This is another form of database marketing that allows companies to send very specific material to target segments.

- **New software languages** are allowing eCommerce applications to be developed faster and more economically. Many people will have heard of languages such as Java which are being used to write eCommerce applications. The individual languages are less important than the fact that they are available and enable the faster development of the market.

Growth in other service industries is facilitating eCommerce

There has also been growth in the development of organisations called Internet service providers (ISPs) such as America Online (AOL) and BT which can provide businesses with access to the Internet and World Wide Web. Combined with a host of companies which specialise in the development of Web sites, it is easier than ever for companies to go on-line. The success of package delivery organisations such as DHL, Federal Express and United Parcel Service (UPS) now means that there are fast, cheap alternative ways of delivering physical products to customers.

Security is a major issue but steps are being taken to address it

The issue of security of transactions that are conducted over a network that is open to everybody and owned by no one individual has given rise to fears of fraud and has held back the growth of the Internet as a major consumer sales channel. The first electronic payments for products and services over the Internet were conventional ones. Subscribers transferred monthly fees for a service from their bank accounts into the account of the selling party in a traditional fashion – by cheque, direct debit or by credit card in a subsequent telephone call. No payments were conducted over the Internet. However, such payments are expensive and can take a long time to process. Subsequent developments include the use of credit cards over the Internet which enable faster and cheaper payments but with the inherent danger of transmitting credit card details over a worldwide network which could be accessed by anybody. Criminals regularly scan the Internet for credit card number details. The use of encryption of credit card details has not provided a complete solution to this problem. In March 1997, the two major credit card organisations, VISA and Mastercard, along with IBM and others, released an agreed technical standard for safeguarding credit card purchases made over open networks such as the Internet. This standard, known as SET (Secure Electronic Transactions) provides robust encryption and identity verification throughout the on-line payment process between the consumer, online merchant and bank, helping consumers to feel safe making purchases over the Internet. The SET protocol is being implemented in the US, Europe and Asia. In Japan, a similar version has been helped with the aid of a $300 million dollar grant from the Japanese government.

INSIGHT: Sweden is an ideal market for Internet banking: it has the highest PC penetration in Europe and its sparse population means bank branches are often few and far between. Nevertheless, the success of S-E Banken's Internet service in attracting 60 000 customers since its launch in December 1996 has taken even the bank by surprise. Security is one of the biggest concerns in Internet banking. With a dial-up PC system, the number of entry points to the system is limited and distribution of the proprietary software can be controlled. On the Internet, the bank is accessible by any Web browser. 'It's not at issue

---

whether the Internet is secure or not – because clearly it is not,' says Mr
Anders Lindqvist, Internet service director at the bank. S-E Banken has
employed a series of security measures to prevent unauthorised access to
customers' accounts but is understandably unwilling to describe them in detail.

Part 2

HOW CAN BUSINESSES CREATE VALUE USING eCOMMERCE?

5

Understand how eCommerce creates value

The concept of eCommerce changes the way companies create value. It can put more power in the hands of customers by making product and price information from different suppliers easier to reach and easier to compare. It can also reduce the cost of doing business, by eliminating or shortening process cycles. eCommerce can create value in three different ways (*see* Figure 5.1):

- it can create new products and services;

- it can create new markets;

- it can enable new business processes.

Figure 5.1
Creation of value through eCommerce

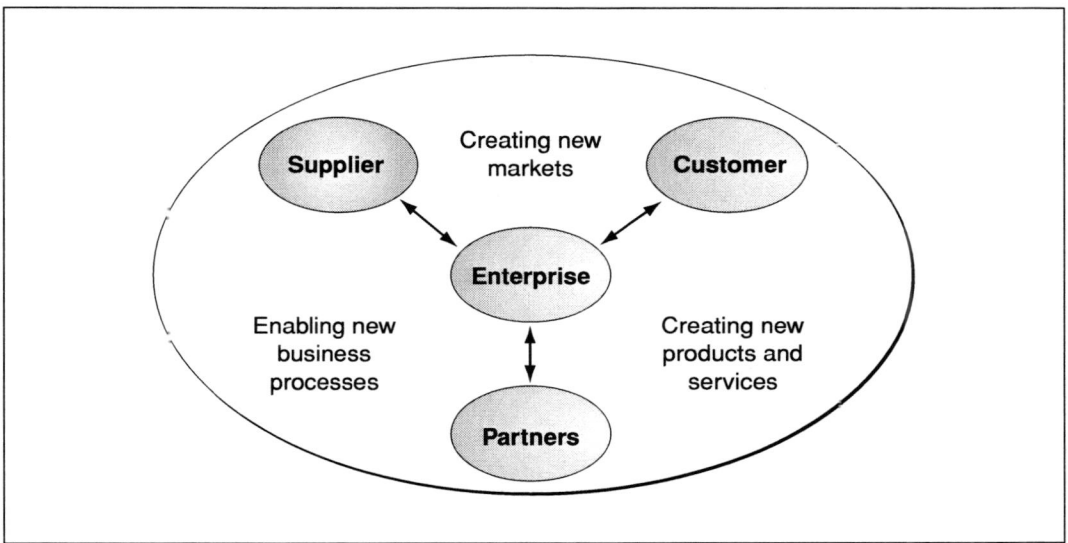

Creating new products and services

The development of the Internet has resulted in the creation of new products and services. Most of these new products and services have a large technology component. Examples of pure technology-driven services include on-line information search engines such as Yahoo! and software products that retrieve and display personalised news information. Examples of other services where technology is a component include on-line financial services for managing bank accounts or trading shares. As Internet and Web-based technologies continue to develop and mature,

more and more of these new products and services will come on stream. In retailing, many traditional products will come under threat as new retailing concepts are tested and commercialised. For example, the ability to download audio, video and software from the Internet will allow consumers to migrate from the traditional physical CDs and video products that they currently purchase.

In addition, eCommerce also provides the ability for customers to participate *directly* in the design of products and services.

In order to fully grasp the range of services which are provided on the Internet, senior managers need to take the time out to browse or 'surf' the Web. What becomes immediately obvious is the sheer scale of information and products and services being offered. This scale and the difficulty of differentiating products and services is one of the many challenges facing organisations trying to develop eCommerce offerings.

Creating new markets

One of the best examples of this is General Electric's Trading Process Network (TPN), a Web-based market where suppliers compete for GE contracts (*see* the Case study 3.1 at the end of Chapter 3). Direct interaction with customers and the creation of stronger relationships is a major area of opportunity. eCommerce creates greater customer intimacy by individualising responses to customer demand.

At this point, it is worth introducing the *extranet*, a type of electronic network which links companies to their trading partners over the Internet. Extranets enable partners to access internal information such as insurance rates, customer accounts, etc., or to link several organisations together into one protected network. They are the successors to the old EDI networks and already account for a significant proportion of business-to-business eCommerce.

INSIGHT: As well as its Web sites which are open to the general public, Dell has also created customised extranet sites for its largest corporate customers to simplify procurement and support processes. One large Fortune 500 customer estimates the annual savings to be more than $2 million from its Dell-developed site, according to Dell. Similarly, Mobil's extranet allows the oil giant to accept purchase orders from 300 separate distributors over the World Wide Web. Ford Motor's new 'FocalPt' extranet supports automobile sales and services from cradle to grave. The extranet is designed to give the 15 000 Ford dealers worldwide a unified system to aid in sales, product promotions and customer service.

The use of the Internet, or extranets, to create new markets can be thought of as a move from the physical marketplace to one which is virtual. Within any industry, some forms of activity are more likely to be virtualised, and virtualised more quickly, than others. In the coming years, eCommerce is likely to be taken up first and adapted more quickly in industries in the upper right quadrant of the model shown in Figure 5.2.

Figure 5.2
Prospects for virtualisation

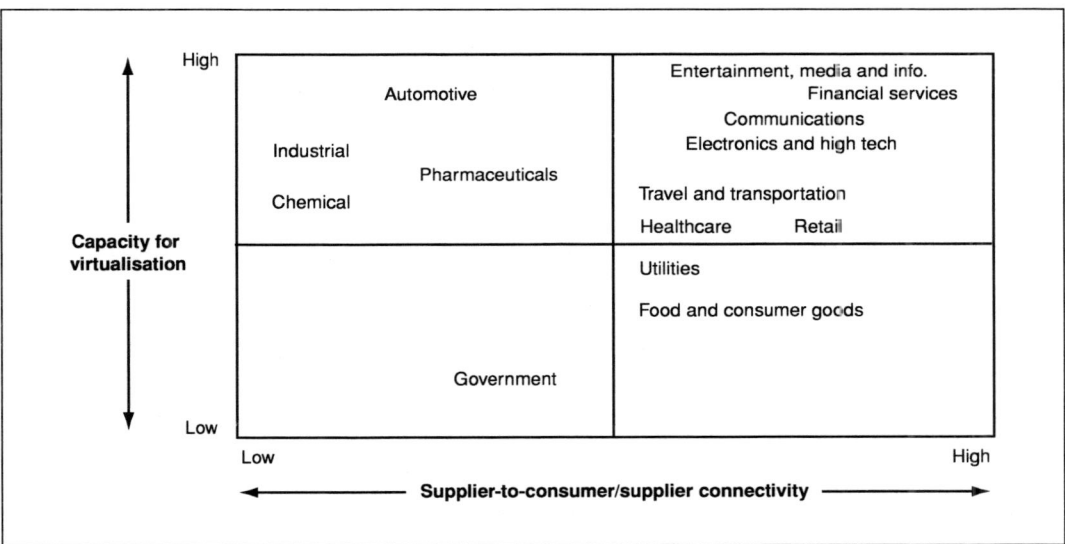

This model is not all-inclusive. While eCommerce will ultimately impact all markets to some extent, immediate opportunities are in those segments where business-to-business or business-to-consumer connectivity (or both) are high, and where the value exchanged is easily 'virtualised'. For example, the food industry may have some network infrastructure but food itself is hard to virtualise, so immediate

opportunities are likely to be limited. We can expect eCommerce in the financial services industry, on the other hand, to be more advanced and dynamic: this market demonstrates extensive connectivity and financial instruments are readily virtualised.

In summary, the types of products and services that are likely to sell successfully in the virtual world are:

- **Catalogue sales.** The catalogue sales model is one that migrates naturally to the Internet. Already, most of the large mail order firms have moved onto the Internet.

- **Brand name goods.** Brand name goods are especially conducive to sales over the Internet. Consumers know the quality of the brand they are buying which is an important point when you cannot touch, feel or try out the product.

- **Product samples.** Products that can be viewed or sampled over the Internet will be successful. Music is one example: a shopper can listen to pieces of songs on a CD before deciding to order it, or snippets of music can be sent as e-mail attachments.

- **Information-intensive products** such as fine wines. Fine wine was traditionally sold in small to medium-sized stores with knowledgeable salespeople to help the usually bewildered consumer. However, big retailers now dominate the market due to volume buying power and companies like Virtual Vineyards in the US and Sainsbury's WineDirect in the UK have muscled in on the fine wine business: their Web sites educate shoppers and then sell them the wine of their choice.

- **Convenience services.** Services and products such as greeting cards and flowers sell relatively well on the Internet. In time, local food delivery might become another niche market; for example, a single Web site could offer menus for all participating restaurants in a particular locality.

- **Digital goods.** Digital goods are ideal for eCommerce. Buyers can take immediate delivery at the time of purchase, providing instant gratification and peace of mind. Digital goods include information such as news, research or data and graphic media like art and photography.

- **Large selections of goods.** On-line stores can have 'virtual inventories' with a depth that would be impossible or prohibitively expensive to duplicate in the physical world. Amazon.com is the best example of this category of electronic retailer: they carry a range of over 2 million book titles.

Enabling new business processes

If implemented correctly, eCommerce can integrate different parts of the supply chain (buyers, sellers, carriers, agents, etc.), slashing inventory costs, reducing lead times and driving down procurement costs in the process. For example, Hilton Hosiery, an Australian division of Sara Lee, now interacts directly with retailers to determine its inventory needs. Order errors have been reduced, and Hilton Hosiery is able to monitor market trends which in turn allows it to plan production more accurately and manage inventory levels to better effect. By enabling a better understanding between provider and customer, eCommerce can also increase customer retention, uncover new selling opportunities and reduce the cost of doing business.

Shell Oil uses a group consolidation system (CERES) to better manage the quarterly results, annual plans and forecasts for its 300 operating companies around the world. Advance Bank, a virtual bank launched by one of Germany's largest financial institutions, outsources back-office functions and investment management processes. As a result, it avoids the high costs associated with physical branch networks and delivers a highly attractive combination of service quality and convenience.

Production and delivery of physical goods (as opposed to pure services) will remain physical events. However, the 'how' and 'when' processes of production and delivery will be affected by the high degree of customisation and customer choice that can be delivered by eCommerce. The delivery of groceries can be timed for the customer's convenience. Service manuals, updates, 'handy hints', customer discussion groups – all may be made accessible to customers via eCommerce *anywhere* and *any time*. This can mean businesses operating extended hours, perhaps 24 hours a day, 365 days a year, which may in turn may lead to further automation of these processes to reduce cost.

Procurement functions can be profoundly affected. New payment systems allow low-value transactions to be processed cheaply; intelligent agents can search for the best prices for the items to be procured. This may lead to automation of the entire procurement process from quotation through to delivery of the goods. Payment over the Internet is another area of significant development which will streamline the payment and settlement functions and processes, reducing the time taken and resources required for these functions.

There is also another type of network which supports eCommerce. While the Internet is a global public medium for linking different businesses and individuals, there are also private versions of the Internet which are not accessible to the general public. *Intranets* are closed network systems that are based on Internet technology. They are isolated within an organisation and used primarily for internal services and communication. They provide a popular platform for knowledge management systems and e-mail. Intranets are frequently connected to the external Internet through a security feature known as a 'firewall' that prevents unauthorised access to the intranet from the outside.

INSIGHT: One of the biggest users of intranets is the Swiss Bank Corporation. In fact it has so many – around a 100 – that it has just appointed a head of intranets to co-ordinate them all. They use intranets for:

- corporate accounting and credit information;
- publishing research internally (and to a select group of 50 external clients);
- trading information;
- ordering information technology equipment;
- IT project management;
- informing staff of regulatory changes.

Because the focus is more on internal communications and dissemination of corporate information around the organisation, intranets have only a relatively minor role to play in eCommerce. However, they do offer significant benefits by improving communication and knowledge sharing within a company. They also provide organisations with the skills, experience and capabilities to move into eCommerce. In a recent survey of marketing and IT professionals, respondents said the type of Website that yielded the greatest return for their company was an intranet (34 per cent), followed by an extranet (29 per cent) and a public Web site (25 per cent). The returns are from improved communications rather than increased sales but an intranet also provides a good introduction to the on-line world and a good starting point for real eCommerce.

CASE STUDY 5.1: The Gap goes on-line in the UK

The Gap

The Gap is a major retailing organisation which has sales of £6 billion worldwide. It is going on-line in the UK, having already established an on-line business in the US in 1997.

Business processes

From The Gap's Web site, on-line shoppers are presented with pictures of a wide variety of clothing items. Details on price, fabric and size are accessed by clicking on the items. If a consumer decides to purchase they simply click on the item and it is added to their 'shopping bag'. Before they confirm their order they have the opportunity to delete or change items. Payment is made by entering credit card details onto the screen. Customers have a choice of selecting overnight or standard delivery. After confirming their orders, customers are sent a confirmation e-mail by The Gap within 24 hours. This direct model provides The Gap with real-time information on orders as well as immediate feedback on sales trends in different lines. With more detailed customer information, it will also allow a more accurate picture of The Gap's customer segments to be analysed.

The process which The Gap uses is also being utilised by many other on-line organisations and is illustrated in Figure 5.3.

Issues

One of the biggest issues that The Gap, and other international retail chains, face as they go on-line is how to manage their pricing policy. This is a challenge faced by many international organisations that charge different prices worldwide. The Web is a worldwide medium, but many organisations price their goods differently from store to store and from region to region (not to mention from one country to another).

Figure 5.3
The Gap's on-line customer service processes

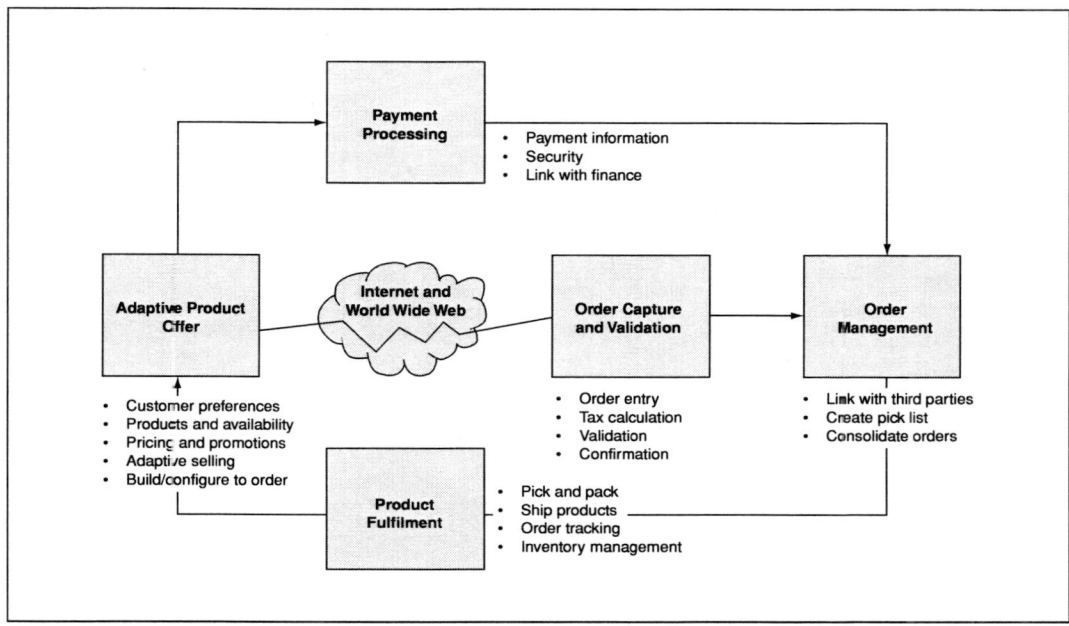

CASE STUDY 5.2: 'Hall of Failures'

We mentioned at the beginning of this briefing that cyberspace is full of failed eCommerce ventures. It is worth taking a quick tour of some of the more notable of these failures to see if we can learn any lessons from their demise:

- **World Avenue**, an extensive 'super-mall' on the Internet, was set up and operated by IBM in 1996. World Avenue was shut down on 9 July 1997 after considerable losses because its 'content' failed to generate enough traffic through the site. Note that not all 'super-malls' have failed – the problems arise from not understanding what it takes to generate traffic and retain customers.

- **1 800 Music Now**, a music CD site, was shut down for two main reasons: high cost of sales generation and active resistance from suppliers.

- **Pathfinder**, from Time Warner, was regarded as an Internet leader with good content from well-known brand names such as *Sports Illustrated* and *Time*. However, undifferentiated targeting of consumers, poor navigation and layout, and a revenue model that was unsustainable created extensive losses and a major reorganisation in April 1997.

- **Nets Inc.** was an on-line marketplace for a variety of industrial goods but filed for Chapter 11 bankruptcy protection and laid off 200 employees. Nets Inc. failed to demonstrate a clear focused approach towards a targeted community of consumers. Again, the concept is not fundamentally flawed – just the execution.

- **Argos**, a UK retailer, failed to understand the consumer buying process in cyberspace and sold a total of only 22 items from its Web site in one ten-month period.

Despite the fact that their eCommerce ventures did not succeed, the owners have probably salvaged some very useful, if expensive, lessons from them. Hopefully, the above case studies and company profiles will also crystallise some of the key messages about what companies need to do (and avoid) if they are to be successful on the Internet.

6

Decide the level of eCommerce at which to operate

There are four levels of eCommerce, with increasing costs and benefits as one moves from one level to the next as shown in Figure 6.1.

Figure 6.1
Levels of eCommerce

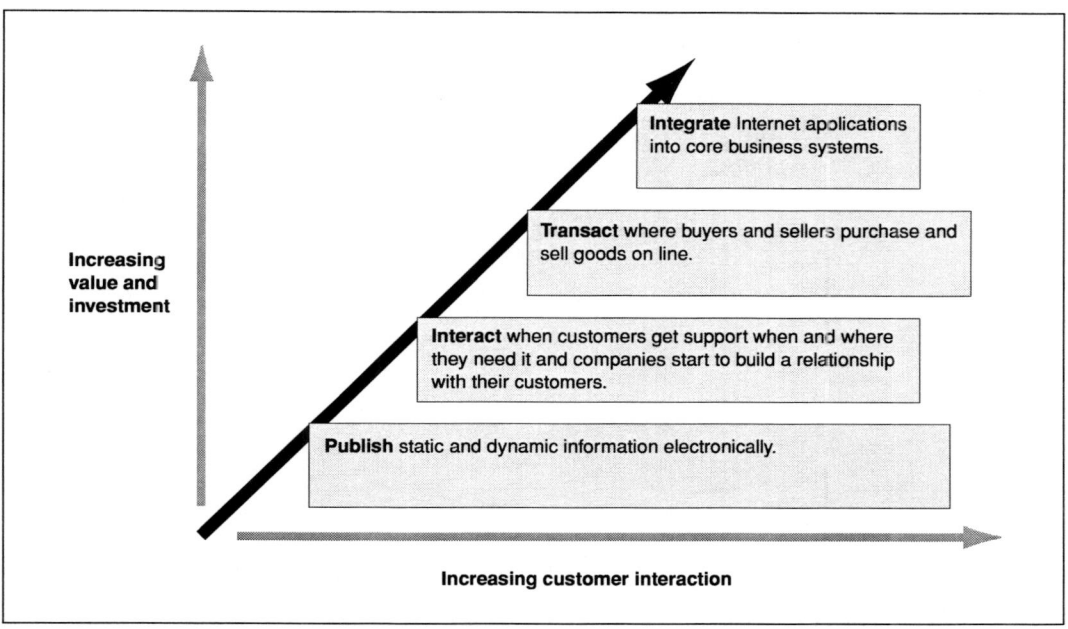

Publish: the first level provides one-way communication only

The first level refers to knowledge dissemination and one-way communication to the consumer. The majority of organisations that have established Web sites have not moved beyond this level. These organisations use the Web to publish company information such as:

• shareholder information such as annual reports and company accounts;

• press releases and other public relations material;

• information on products and services for customers;

• details of recruitment opportunities for potential employees;

• general advertising.

> **INSIGHT:** A 1998 global survey of 100 large publicly traded companies was critical of most corporate Web sites – all but three companies (AT&T, Bell Atlantic and Sun Microsystems) were too narrowly focused on one type of visitor and were unable to provide 'content' for investors, customers and potential employees alike. Other criticisms included poor layout and navigation making it difficult for visitors to find their way around the Web sites, and overuse of graphics making it slow to download information.

The process of designing and creating a Web site is known as 'authoring' and good authoring practices include the provision of good navigation around the site, details of when each page was last updated, cross-links to other pages and other Web sites, and so on. It is not the intention of this briefing to examine in detail the variety of good and bad authoring practices. Suffice it to say that there are many excellent Web design companies that can design Web sites at reasonable prices. Smaller organisations can cut costs by carrying out their own design (if they have the skills in-house) but for most companies the choice is obvious – use a good external Web design company.

In general, it should be noted that 'publishing' rarely constitutes effective Internet commerce – it is merely a one-way flow of information from the supplier to the customer. Yet this is exactly the level at which most organisations have launched themselves into cyberspace. By mid-1998, there were more than 300 million pages on the World Wide Web – proof not only that companies are willing to invest in Web 'publishing' but also that the sheer variety of Web sites to visit makes it almost impossible to stand out in the crowd.

> **MANAGEMENT TIP:** If you're a large organisation, move beyond the 'publish' level.
>
> There has been a lot of criticism recently about the number of large blue-chip companies who have boring and uninformative Web sites, or where the design, layout and navigation are not customer-friendly. Poor Web design and lack of 'content' should not be acceptable for blue-chip organisations, and most such companies can afford to move to at least the second level of eCommerce, where the benefits are greater for relatively little additional cost.

Interact: the second level has two-way information flows

The second level of Internet commerce refers to collaboration and interactive engagement with the customer on the Internet. The greater the level of engagement, the greater the likelihood that the Web site will attract visitors back to your site again and again. For example, Dell Computer's Web site features on-line technical support services that include detailed reference information on all Dell products, self-diagnostic tools and e-mail links to on-line technical support representatives. The company further provides its customers access to the same product information used by the company's technical support personnel through an on-line archive of 35 000 items dating back to the era of the Intel 8088 processor.

The most important aspect of any Internet site is to provide good 'content' which is of value to the particular customers you are trying to attract to your site. Content can come in many different forms:

- self-generated where the company decides to share some of its own information with the customer, e.g. research material or back editions of newspapers or magazines that have been indexed for ease of access, applications that allow customers to design and price their own products or constantly updated information of how products can be used;
- commissioned or bought in from a third party that specialises in generating 'content' for Web sites;
- generated by customers in the form of reviews and discussion groups;
- generated by third parties that are linked to your Web site.

MANAGEMENT TIP: Give your customers something for nothing.

Otherwise they won't come. For example, Guinness received an extraordinary hit-rate on its Web site by allowing visitors to download a PC screensaver based on a very successful television advertising campaign. *The Economist*'s Web site allows customers access to two years of back editions of their weekly magazine, as well a screensaver with world time, future world events and detailed statistical analysis of 60 countries.

If you can generate traffic through your site, you have the basis for effective eCommerce through one or more of the following:

- sales revenue created indirectly as a result of customers visiting your site and then purchasing your goods or services through existing channels;

- referral fees from other Web sites to which you have introduced some of your on-line customers;

- advertising revenues from third parties that buy space on your Web site.

However, if you are really interested in selling your goods and services over the Internet, you will need to move to the third level of electronic commerce.

Transact: the third level is where true eCommerce begins

A much more advanced level of eCommerce involves the buying and selling of goods over the Internet, with an associated exchange of payment. This is true Internet commerce and the potential benefits for buyers and sellers are enormous, if implemented properly. For example, about 225 000 customers visit Dell Computer's Web site each week, where they can electronically design, price and purchase computer systems.

However, moving to the 'transact' level of Internet commerce is not without its risks. For a start, the costs of establishing a fully integrated transaction-processing Web site are significant. As we will see in Chapter 7, the costs of building and operating a 'transact' site may run as high as several million pounds for the initial investment, not to mention the additional operating costs that may be incurred.

Moving your organisation to the 'transact' level will also typically require a number of significant changes to:

- **organisational structure** to ensure that the eCommerce venture has the correct level of support, autonomy and devolved decision-making power that it will require, and that responsibility for the management of the eCommerce venture is properly integrated with the organisation's other channels of distribution;

- **underlying processes** for marketing and sales, order entry, procurement and distribution – this may necessitate rebuilding the entire value chain for the organisation;

- **technical infrastructure** to allow customers access to the organisation's systems 24 hours a day, seven days a week, 365 days a year;

- **skills and human resources**, both for managing a radically new distribution channel and for managing the expectations of the people currently working in the organisation's existing distribution channels.

> **INSIGHT:** Many computer systems in organisations operate in a 'batch' mode. In other words, transactions are batched up during the day and the batch program is run for a number of hours overnight. This means that the company's main computer systems may not be accessible 24 hours a day – a major problem for a 'transact' eCommerce operation which requires a so-called '24 × 7' model (available 24 hours a day, seven days a week). It may be in the middle of the night where the computer system sits, but the customer can be sitting in any time zone.

Most companies will seek outside assistance in dealing with some or all of these changes. Typically, consultants are used for the technical and process elements but it may be necessary to seek assistance with the organisational and human resources issues as well. We will examine how to approach these changes later in this briefing.

Integrate: the fourth level involves stronger relationships with trading partners

The final level of eCommerce can be regarded as an extension to the 'transact' level. In the 'integrate' level, the computer systems and processes of the buyers and sellers are integrated to form a much stronger formalised relationship between the trading partners. In many cases, this involves the creation of a business-to-business extranet which links the trading partners in a secure environment over the Internet. Moving through the different levels of eCommerce to the 'transact' or 'integrate' levels provides companies with a structured method of achieving the levels of integration

between trading partners that was originally envisaged for EDI. In theory, operating at the 'integrate' level is a more complete version of the old EDI model. In practice, many of the issues and difficulties of implementation remain the same.

CASE STUDY 6.1: First Financial Services

First Financial Services is a (real but disguised) UK financial services company with more than two million customers which operates primarily through a network of more than 500 branches. Its primary products include two types of current account, a choice of deposit accounts and loan products including personal loans and home mortgages. In 1995, it launched a basic telephone banking service which was low-cost and proved very popular. The customers who used the service were younger, more affluent and generally more profitable than the average branch-based customer. On the basis of its successful telephone banking service, First Financial Services decided in 1996 to pilot an Internet-based service as well.

The First Internet pilot

Tom Wray, a senior IT manager, was put in charge of the project and a cross-functional project team assembled. After 11 months of design and systems development effort, an Internet service was launched at the beginning of 1997 to a selected group of 1000 customers, including bank staff. On the basis of favourable reaction from this pilot group, the service was quickly extended to all customers during the summer of 1997.

The First Internet service

The First Internet service was aimed at both individual customers and small businesses that wanted to manage their accounts on-line. The concept was not new to commercial customers who were already used to a 'Minitel' version of the service in the mid-1990s. First Internet allowed a number of basic transactions to be carried out including balances to be viewed, cash to be transferred from one account to another and bills to be paid. It also provided information on First Financial Services' core deposit and loan products, and allowed personal customers to apply for personal loans and mortgages over the Internet. In addition to providing information

on products and services, the Web site also contained a number of pages which described the company, its mission and objectives, its financial results and job opportunities that were currently available within the organisation. The site contained a relatively small amount of 'content' but First Financial Services was aware that a competitor's Web site, which provided information and analysis of sporting fixtures and results from the national football league (which it sponsored) was likely to attract more visitors than its own offering.

The launch of the Internet service was supported by a major marketing campaign which piggy-backed off a £1 million advertising campaign for First Financial Services' personal loans. Tom Wray and the senior management of the bank had high expectations from the service.

The results

Initial take-up among the target personal customer base was good. It appealed to the same younger, affluent customers who had been attracted to the telephone banking service two years previously. First Internet was flooded with thousands of applications in the first three months of operation. Additional staff were taken on to process all the applications, and the service held up well despite initial fears that the volume of enquiries might overwhelm the system. By January 1998, the customer base stood at over 7000 customers although new customer applications were beginning to dwindle to less than 25 a day. Reaction from commercial customers was also very positive as the service met many of their needs for basic cash management and it was pushed with enthusiasm by the account managers.

However, a number of issues also arose which began to erode the confidence of senior management in the venture. Ongoing costs were more than twice the original estimates in the business plan for the level of hits received by the site. Analysis of the total Internet customer base showed that less that 500 personal customers were regular users (i.e. visited the Web site at least twice in the past month) of the First Internet service. At least 3200 personal customers who signed up for the service had either never used it or had only used it once. Moreover, the major marketing campaign for the service, which was supposed to be driven by branch staff, failed to materialise as it was perceived that the new service was cannibalising existing sales and having a detrimental impact on branch profitability which was the primary

measure of branch performance. A small number of personal mortgage leads were generated and followed up by branch staff and a paltry number of personal loans were booked through the Internet service.

Customer research

Customer research was conducted which identified some major barriers to success:

- a very cumbersome and manual registration process, which had been designed to provide added security for the customer's benefit but which managed to put customers off the service even before they tried it;

- a strong preference by customers to phone the telephone banking service rather than dial into the Internet service because the telephone was a much quicker and more efficient medium for most of the basic transactions that customers wanted to perform;

- a major overestimation of the sales potential of the Internet service for personal finance coupled with a lack of understanding of how the Internet could be used in the sales process (this was exacerbated by the reluctance of branch staff to promote a competing service to 'their' customers).

When the results of the pilot study were re-analysed, it also transpired that the favourable reaction came from commercial customers and from bank staff who were incentivised to use the service in return for their feedback. The reaction from 'real' customers was more circumspect and the subsequent poor response from personal customers was consistent with the messages that should have been learned from the pilot.

Lessons learned

In comparison to the earlier telephone-based service, First Internet was regarded internally within First Financial Services as something of a flop. Despite the pain, First Financial Services did learn some valuable lessons from the First Internet experience, including:

- the need for a business case and implementation plan with clearly defined objectives which could be used to monitor the success of the initial pilot service;

- that a 'me-too' offering is no substitute for thinking through what customers really wanted from an Internet-based service;

- that an ability to generate and sustain traffic at the Web site by creating a community of interested and loyal customers was critical to achieving sales targets;

- that senior branch management should have been involved in the design, management and roll-out of the service, rather than devolving responsibility to a team of technical experts with input from some middle-ranking business representatives.

The experiences of First Financial Services are not uncommon. Most companies introduce an Internet service as an additional sales or service channel to their existing operations and then grapple with the issues of integrating them with their existing business. The cynics might argue that the First Internet service was a financial and public relations disaster. The optimists will put it down to experience and argue that first-hand experience of problems with the Internet is invaluable in creating the next generation of on-line services. In truth, both are right.

Part 3

HOW DO YOU IMPLEMENT AN eCOMMERCE SOLUTION?

7

Start by building a sound business case

The business case for eCommerce can be made in different ways, ranging from 'Everyone else is doing it, so why aren't we?' through to formal business cases based on return-on-investment calculations. Typically, the majority fall into the former category, with vague promises of increased sales, improved customer service or reduced costs, without any clear strategy for achieving the savings. The lack of a convincing business case and clear business strategy is often the reason senior managers are disappointed by the returns from eCommerce initiatives.

While business cases differ from situation to situation and from company to company, most contain the same key elements (*see* the sample business case at the end of this chapter for reference):

- **background**, describing the imperatives for embarking on a venture into eCommerce;

- **customer proposition**, stressing the value to the customer of the venture – as we have already mentioned, this is the most important element of any business plan;

- **financials**, showing clearly the impact that the initiative will have on both costs and revenues;

- **assumptions**, underpinning the financial projections – in particular, assumptions on sales projections must be comprehensive and convincing;

- **action/implementation issues**, ranging from technology and process changes through to the recruitment of additional skills and competencies required to make the venture a success;

- **management**, stating clearly the expectations of senior management sponsorship and support for the initiative to make it work.

As a senior business manager, you are more likely to be on the receiving end of a business plan than be the creator of one. If any of the first four key elements shown above is missing from the business plan, the plan itself is probably flawed. The plan may not have addressed the final two items in any great detail but, when evaluating such a business plan, you will need to be convinced that these elements are in place. In particular, you will need to understand who is going to be held responsible for the success of this initiative and whether they have the right skills and resources at their

disposal. In reviewing the business plan, pay particular attention to the financials and the underlying assumptions. In particular, keep the following points in mind:

- eCommerce ventures often involve significant investments and long payback periods;

- sales projections are usually overestimated (and ongoing costs underestimated);

- reductions in operating costs are achievable but difficult to realise;

- intangible benefits such as improved customer service should not be ignored.

Let us examine each of these in turn.

An eCommerce venture often involves significant investment and a long payback period

A modest investment of less than £50 000 will allow most companies to establish a basic presence on the Internet. However, this investment is wasted if nobody visits your site in cyberspace. And the truth of the matter is that nobody will, if you don't make it attractive for them to visit and if you don't advertise your site heavily. Moreover, if you decide to establish anything other than a basic presence, your initial investment costs will rise dramatically – perhaps to the order of several million pounds for a 'transact' operation, primarily on technology hardware and software, implementation support and launch costs. However, this level of investment is a prerequisite to engaging in true eCommerce.

Many executives fail to understand that the serious eCommerce players are buying market share at the expense of short-term profits. These organisations are playing a strategic game and positioning themselves to succeed in the longer term, even if the short-term benefits are not immediately obvious. Adopting such a stance requires deep pockets and steady nerves. Building a business case which downplays the initial investment costs in order to show a quicker payback may appear an attractive option but may ultimately lead to failure. The overall message is that senior managers need to be realistic about what is required to play the eCommerce game.

MANAGEMENT TIP: Don't expect to make early profits from business-to-consumer eCommerce ventures.

Even with the right customer proposition, the right business processes and the right organisational structure, it is likely to take considerable time for your eCommerce venture to move into the black. One of the most successful eCommerce companies, Amazon.com, has still to make a profit despite being valued at more than $2 billion. Eighteen months after opening for business, Amazon.com recorded losses of $5 m on revenues of $12 m. In 1997, Amazon lost nearly $30 m on revenues of nearly $150 m, proving that even the most successful business-to-consumer ventures can take years to become profitable.

Sales projections are usually overestimated (and ongoing costs underestimated)

Forecasting future sales is always a tricky process. In business-to-business eCommerce initiatives where trading partners are bound by contractual obligations, it may be possible to achieve greater predictability of sales. The business-to-consumer market is very different. Many companies have simply assumed that their existing sales process can be translated directly into cyberspace. It cannot. The entire market offering and proposition to the customer needs to be redeveloped to make it work in cyberspace. The type of customer that buys from the Internet is different to a customer who walks into a shop. New approaches to customer segmentation, product offerings and sales processes are required.

INSIGHT: A European eCommerce initiative set up in 1997 was eChristmas, sponsored primarily by Hewlett-Packard, Microsoft and United Parcel Service (UPS). Twenty-two Internet service providers (ISPs) and 18 solution developers hosted and built merchant store sites, bringing them on-line in one integrated environment. At the end of the project, 140 merchants in nine European countries offered a range of 1800 goods available for purchase over the Internet. Total sales over the Christmas period? A mere 350 purchases.

While the sales results may have been disappointing, the objectives of the eChristmas initiative mentioned above were to understand more about consumer purchasing behaviour as well as to sell products. Perhaps the greatest mistake in making assumptions of consumer on-line sales is failing to understand the consumer buying process. Customers don't simply buy. They go through a series of stages which eventually culminates in the actual purchase. Companies need to have a very clear understanding of how an Internet presence can help them meet customers' needs through each of these buying stages. In the final analysis, there is no substitution for consumer trials and pilots to allow the proposition to be adapted, tweaked and modified until it really does meet the consumer's needs.

It is surprising how many companies fail to realise that there are significant ongoing costs that must be borne, even if the investment does not extend much beyond a basic Web site. Market research carried out in 1996 found that UK companies spent an average of more than £22 000 a year on their Web sites, and that this investment was soon expected to increase to an average of £56 000 a year. More recent figures indicate that high-profile sites with good well-updated content and full transactional capabilities will cost £1 000 000 a year or more to operate, with the major categories of ongoing cost likely to be as shown in Table 7.1.

Table 7.1
Ongoing costs of running a Web site

Cost category	% total costs	Typical items of expenditure
Staff	35	Programmers, customer service representatives, content developers, creative designers, management
Content development	25	The written material, graphics or research that generates traffic through the site
Processing	20	Processing costs of ordering goods
Marketing	10	Advertising and brand development
Technology	10	Hardware and software upgrades and maintenance

While the exact split of costs will differ from site to site – for example, some companies will choose to spend significantly more on advertising and brand development to establish a strong foothold in the market – the figures in Table 7.1 should give an estimate of where your money is being, or should be, spent.

Reductions in operating costs are achievable but difficult to realise

Companies can achieve cost savings through eCommerce but it is not always easy to realise these savings. For example, a leading bank correctly identified that paper-based transactions such as cheques and staff-assisted transactions such as cash withdrawals and balance enquiries at the branch counter were expensive and were distracting staff from other customer service or sales functions. So far, so good. However, the addition of an Internet service increased the bank's cost base. When the Internet service was launched, the bank failed to displace transactions and costs from the existing branch channel. No serious initiatives were put in place to change customer behaviour, staff levels were allowed to remain at the old levels and none of the existing branches were closed. Even when the bank finally managed to change customer behaviour through pricing, training, customer incentives and reduction of service levels in the branch, the overall number of transactions per customer increased as customers found it more convenient to use the newer channels.

> **MANAGEMENT TIP:** Be ruthless about managing your overall channel costs when you go on-line.
>
> Beware of surveys that conclude that 'the cost of a typical bank transaction in a branch is £1 compared to a little more than 50 pence for telephone banking, around 25 pence for an ATM transaction and less than 10 pence for a transaction over the Internet'. Here's why. While a greenfield eCommerce initiative requires less infrastructure and fewer physical assets, senior executives have to view direct channels such as the telephone or the Internet as additional channels to be managed in conjunction with traditional channels such as stores, sales forces, distributors and wholesalers. Despite lower transaction costs, moving onto the Internet will increase a company's overall cost base unless cost is ruthlessly taken out of existing channels.

In the case of business-to-business eCommerce, the potential benefits can be significant and in some instances can help companies reduce their total expenditure by as much as 10–15 per cent. The majority of these savings come from increased supplier leverage and improved compliance with corporate procurement contracts, with the remainder coming from productivity improvements and error reduction. However, these cost reductions can prove difficult to drive out and can only be achieved through hard negotiation with suppliers typically involving giving more business to those suppliers (sometimes single-sourcing from that supplier) in return for price reductions.

Fewer physical assets are also required to operate an Internet service. Going back to our example of the bank, the introduction of an Internet service should have allowed the bank to reduce its physical network of branches and other supporting infrastructure. Some companies have taken the concept even further, by adopting a policy of outsourcing all 'non-core' operations. Companies such as Microsoft have benefited from such an approach through the additional flexibility it offers them as the market changes.

> **INSIGHT:** Over the years, Microsoft has increased its policy of outsourcing. In the past, its 'factories' produced boxes of computer discs, CD-ROMs and manuals for operating its software. Nowadays, 'factories' are outsourced to third parties, allowing Microsoft greater flexibility to increase or decrease production and respond to a rapidly changing marketplace. Many of Microsoft's corporate customers sign licensing agreements which allow them to distribute Microsoft software electronically within their organisations, while individual consumers can download software upgrades over the Internet.

Intangible benefits such as improved customer service should not be ignored

There are other intangible benefits which, by their very nature, are difficult to quantify. In some circumstances, a strong case can be made on the basis of intangible benefits. For example, one of the greatest intangible benefits is improved customer service. An additional service channel which is available 24 hours a day

and which is more likely to be used by the more affluent customer segments may well help to increase loyalty or reduce defections.

In other circumstances, it is justifiable to treat an eCommerce venture as 'research and development'. However, like any R&D expenditure, there must be clear limits on the extent of investment and the time period over which such an investment is made, before senior management decides to commercialise the venture or pull the plug.

And finally, there are purely defensive reasons why companies launch themselves into cyberspace: 'The competition are doing it, and we cannot be left behind.' It is true that the lack of an Internet presence for large organisations can be viewed as a weakness. However, it should not be acceptable to use this as a justification for not producing a business case.

> **MANAGEMENT TIP:** Always produce a business case – even when the benefits are difficult to quantify.
>
> In some ways, the argument for producing a business case when most of the benefits are intangible, are even stronger than when the benefits are easily quantifiable. Even if the business case can only be summarised by 'we need to commit £X m to launch a competitive service and we do not foresee a payback of less than five years' it can be immensely helpful to senior management in making up their own minds how much to invest in the venture. At a minimum, it forces them to think clearly about the justification if they have to take the case to the board for approval. But more importantly, it gives them a frame of reference for evaluating the expenditure and the future returns.

SAMPLE BUSINESS CASE STUDY 7.1:
Executive Summary

Background

In the past two years, our major competitor ABC has first piloted, and then launched, an Internet service. At first we chose to watch and wait, as we were not convinced that the benefits of launching a similar service outweighed the costs. However, we are currently perceived in the marketplace as being 'behind the competition' and some of our most profitable customers have been enquiring about when we are going to launch a similar service. Recent market research has also indicated that a small number of our customers who have defected to the competition have done so solely because they were looking to do business by Internet. Much more worrying is the fact that the majority of these defections have come from our most profitable customer segment, the high net worth sector. We propose that the time is now right for us to launch an Internet service of our own which will defend our position in the high net worth market.

Customer proposition

Over the past six months, we have conducted market research into the type of service that our customers might want. We concentrated on our two most profitable customer segments and ran a series of focus groups to determine what our 'proposition' to those customers should be. The results of the focus groups indicate that our high net worth customers are most interested in an 'out-of-hours' customer service facility which allows them to check the status of their accounts and carry out some basic transactions. There also appears to be strong interest among this customer group in learning more about our products, with a view to making purchases subsequently. We use the phrase 'appears to be' because the research indicates that customers are very willing to use the Internet to research their products but there is still some reluctance to place orders directly over the Internet. The research suggests that the account manager or salesperson is still valued by customers as they make the final decision to purchase the product.

We are therefore proposing an Internet service which will provide customers with 24-hour, 365-day access to their accounts, information on our product range and the

ability to make an appointment with an account manager or salesperson through an e-mail facility. If the service proves popular, we will extend it to a full 'product purchase' Internet site, but in the first instance we will only allow appointments to be made.

Financials and assumptions

We expect the up-front costs of launching the service to amount to £700 000, with an ongoing cost of £500 000 a year thereafter. Both up-front and ongoing figures include a contingency of 20 per cent for unforeseen costs. The payback for the venture is estimated at five years, with an internal rate of return (IRR) of 22 per cent. We have taken a conservative approach to the financials, assuming that no additional sales will arise as a result of this venture. The benefits primarily accrue from our assumption that, if no such service is provided, at least 10 per cent of our high net worth customers will defect to ABC over the next two years, which is consistent with the trend over the past 12 months. In addition, we have assumed that the cost of running our distributor channel will reduce by £400 000 a year and we have specific recommendations on how this will be achieved. In the event that an Internet service does lead, either directly or indirectly, to a 5 per cent increase in sales revenues, the IRR on the venture would increase to 45 per cent. Similarly, if we only achieve half of the cost reduction targets in our distributor channel, the IRR drops to 15 per cent.

Implementation plan and management sponsorship

In this business case, we have included a high-level implementation plan, which assumes an internal project team of three people on a full-time basis for the next 12 months, additional market research to finalise the 'proposition' and implementation support from external consultants. In order to make this venture a success, we recommend that Bill Patton assumes direct responsibility for this venture. Without the direct support of an executive director, we feel that the chances of success are reduced significantly.

8

Apply the guiding principles for successful eCommerce

There are a number of guiding principles that senior executives should bear in mind as they embark on an eCommerce initiative. The primary principles are to:

- always start with your customer proposition;

- think creatively about how to design your key processes;

- commit your best executives;

- create 'value networks' to attract customers;

- leverage your customers and suppliers;

- 'think big, start small and scale quickly'.

Always start with your customer proposition

In most cases, a new customer proposition will be required to be successful in eCommerce. It is simply not good enough to say 'we're going to sell our goods (or procure our raw materials) on the Web'. Traditional sales methods are unlikely to work in cyberspace – consumers' needs and buying behaviours are different and companies must focus on understanding exactly what those differences are. For example, the 'Internet mall' proposition – a single site where customers could purchase a variety of different products – proved to be far less attractive on the Internet than in real life. In real life, a large shopping mall saves time and shoe-leather. The proposition to cybershoppers is less clear (see the 'Hall of Failures' at the end of Chapter 5). Remember that a viable customer proposition is only likely to exist for the types of products described in Chapter 5 as being easy to 'virtualise', e.g. catalogue sales, brand name goods, information-intensive or digital products.

In business-to-business eCommerce, the customer proposition is relatively straightforward – it is primarily about reduced procurement costs (for the buyer) and a greater share of the buyer's wallet (for the seller). The proposition in business-to-consumer eCommerce requires more careful consideration and must incorporate a very clear understanding of how, and why, consumers buy through an electronic medium. For example, Amazon.com's real advantage is its discussion forums, book reviews and services such as Eyes (an e-mail service which informs customers about books that they have expressed an interest in buying). Another example: visitors to The Music Connection's Musicmaker site can mix and match

their own favourite songs on-line and put them all on a single CD – a new proposition for music lovers. The cost for each personalised CD is $9.95 for five tracks and $19.95 for 15 tracks, payable through a secure credit card transaction.

Think creatively about how to redesign your key processes

The customer proposition for a new eCommerce venture will typically differ from the traditional proposition, and this requires many associated processes to change as well. For example, operating at the 'transact' or 'integrate' levels of eCommerce requires integration between the Web site and the 'back office' systems in the company. Without this integration, companies run the risk of allowing customers to order items that are not in stock, pay for items that fail to get delivered or provide information that is different to information provided by the company elsewhere. Several organisations accept orders at their Web sites but then print the same orders and pass them to a data entry clerk who then manually rekeys them into the existing order-entry system. While it may make sense to start an Internet service in this fashion (at least to get a service off the ground), the level of service is likely to degrade quickly and damage the company's reputation.

> **INSIGHT:** An example of not getting the product offer right – the magazine *Business Traveller* went to British Midland's Cyberseat reservations page and was quoted prices of £144 and £89 as the airline's cheapest fares from London to Frankfurt and Paris respectively. A telephone call to the same airline produced quotes of £106 and £69. Needless to say, *Business Traveller* was less than impressed.

Process re-engineering often requires major changes to existing work practices and requires the active involvement and support of existing employees. Do not underestimate the amount of time this can take. An alternative route which many organisations take is to create a greenfield operation and build new processes from scratch. However, even this can take considerable time. For example, Dell has been refining and adapting its direct sales model for well over a decade.

Commit your best executives

In many of the companies where eCommerce initiatives have been implemented successfully, the initiatives are driven either by the chief executive or by a senior executive with an all-consuming passion for making eCommerce work. It is no coincidence that whenever newspapers and magazines report the successes of companies such as Amazon.com, Dell Computers and General Electric, the names of Jeff Bezos (CEO and founder of Amazon), Michael Dell (CEO and founder of Dell) and Harvey Seegers (CEO of GE Information Services) appear prominently.

One of the main reasons for involving your best executives is that some very large bets have to be taken to be successful in eCommerce, particularly when operating at the 'transact' and 'integrate' levels. In business-to-business eCommerce, the entire relationship between a company and its suppliers or its customers will probably undergo dramatic change. This can often only be brokered by the managing director or senior executives. In business-to-consumer eCommerce, major investments and long payback periods are common. Unless the initiative is driven and underwritten by the managing director, there is a real risk the company will quit the initiative before the benefits start to come through.

Create 'value networks' to attract customers

The economics of eCommerce are fundamentally different to traditional commerce. Initial investment, in terms of technology and marketing, can be very high and rapid volume and market share growth are required to recoup the investment. It costs almost the same on an ongoing basis to provide an Internet-based customer service function to 100 000 customers as it does for 1000. But, for many eCommerce operations, a customer base of 100 000 may be the minimum required to pay back the fixed cost of getting the venture off the ground. In a high fixed cost/low variable cost environment, it is vital to reach a critical mass of transactions quickly, and the only guaranteed means of reaching and sustaining critical mass requires a combination of heavy advertising and the creation of on-line communities.

INSIGHT: The economics of eCommerce have been referred to by one commentator as 'Doomonomics', after the hugely successful PC game called Doom. The inventors of Doom decided to operate a slightly different economic model for the pricing of the product – they gave it away for free. As a result, Doom became a worldwide success almost overnight. The payback came from the revenues for subsequent versions of the game and other games manufactured by the same company.

An on-line community is a self-sustaining group of customers that will use your Web site or discussion forum as a meeting place to exchange ideas, comments, gripes and problems – and of course, to buy your products. As companies increase the size of their on-line communities, the benefits increase for the customers as well. The 'network effect' increases the value to each user as the number of customers grows and the size of the on-line communities increases. One of the best examples of the creation of successful on-line communities is Amazon.com. Many of the reviews for the 2.5 million books in Amazon.com's virtual bookstore are provided by Amazon's own customers – a very valuable network effect. Jeff Bezos, who runs Amazon.com, states that the company is actually an information broker, relying on an increasing community of customers, publishers and other associate booksellers to drive up his profits. Amazon's 'associates program' pays the owners of other Web sites an 8 per cent commission on any sales that are directed to its virtual bookshop.

This 'value network' leads to an increasing ability to generate revenue (subscription fees, advertising, product sales) as the size of the network or on-line community grows. For example, when America On-line (AOL) recently bought its loss-making competitor CompuServe, it increased its worldwide subscriber base to around 10 million, thereby increasing the value of its overall network. Customer subscriptions are not the only source of revenues for AOL. Increasingly, AOL is able to charge more for advertising and other services. For example, Tel Save Holdings is paying $100 million to market its phone service on AOL, and 1-800-FLOWERS (an Internet-based version of Interflora) is paying £25 million plus a share of revenue in a four-year deal. Likewise, Amazon.com will pay $19 million over three years for an exclusive link on AOL's browser.

MANAGEMENT TIP: Join forces with a company that has an Internet product that customers can use on your site.

There are several Internet products that could make your site more attractive to your customers. For example, a Swiss Internet company has invented a Web product called the 164 Currency Converter which allows on-line users to translate the values of 164 world currencies. A number of companies now offer this conversion service from their Web sites — it's a 'value network' that makes sense for the consumer, the companies that provide the service on their Web sites and for the people who built the currency conversion software. While this may not constitute a true 'value network', it is at least a step in the right direction.

Leverage your customers and suppliers

Customers can be made to help themselves if there is a benefit in it for them. Even when the benefit is not that apparent, customers can still be persuaded to do what they are told. In the same way that McDonald's found out that their customers could be persuaded to empty and return their trays before leaving the restaurant, companies providing eCommerce services can minimise the workload by persuading their customers to serve themselves. General Motors and Rover enable their customers to design their own cars before they order them. Federal Express, the package delivery company which moves 2.4 million pieces every day, allows its customers to access its package tracking database. By letting 12 000 customers a day click their way through Web pages to pinpoint their parcels — instead of asking a human operator to do it for them — FedEx saves an estimated $2 million a year. Similarly, the package delivery company UPS claims that it saves $200 000 every day by providing customer service over the Internet rather than over the telephone. Moreover, customers can also be persuaded to join in the recruitment of other customers, a technique employed for years at Tupperware parties. However, the economic model for eCommerce means that the benefits in cyberspace are significantly greater than in the sale of plastic boxes.

In business-to-business eCommerce, the focus changes to the leverage that can be applied to suppliers. The concept is no different to the way in which large buyers

negotiate major price reductions from their suppliers in return for a greater share of the market. However, the economic model of eCommerce creates a much greater incentive for applying such leverage. For example, General Electric Lighting's factory in Cleveland needed to order some custom parts to repair their machinery. Although standard practice would have been to send production-line blueprints to a short list of suppliers, this time they posted the specifications and 'requests for quotes' on their Web site – and drew an extra seven unexpected bidders. The winner was a Hungarian company that would not have been contacted in the days of paper purchasing forms. GE Lighting paid just $320 000 for the parts, a 20 per cent saving on the expected cost.

Here again, lessons can be learned from the experiences of companies that have implemented EDI. If you have leverage over your suppliers, it should be used. If your suppliers are of a similar size, or bigger than you, the balance of power swings the other way and clever negotiation skills rather than brute force is the order of the day.

MANAGEMENT TIP: Don't underestimate the backlash from your suppliers.

1 800 Music Now was an Internet site set up by the US telecommunications company MCI to sell compact discs over the Internet. It too was shut down because of the high cost of sales generation and active resistance from suppliers. Unlike the book market, which Amazon.com entered with much success, the music industry is not a fragmented market. It is dominated by half a dozen major organisations such as Sony who are also interested in Internet commerce. They viewed 1 800 Music Now as a direct competitor to be stifled at birth. The results? MCI spent an estimated $40 m promoting the site and its top selling CD sold only 400 units. MCI eventually decided to shut down the operation.

'Think big, start small and scale quickly'

Organisations need to have a clear 'end game' in mind. Michael Dell, the founder of Dell Computers, has stated that he would like to see all of his business being done over the Internet, and has set a target of having 50 per cent of revenues coming from the Internet by the year 2000.

The way eCommerce initiatives are treated should be similar to the way in which new products are developed. Not all eCommerce ideas can be commercialised successfully so it is important to allow many ideas to be tried and the greatest funding applied to the few ventures that show the greatest promise. If an Internet venture is not successful it should be killed off or radically overhauled so that the appropriate returns are driven out of the investment. Typically, this requires responsibility to be devolved to a number of individuals or a small team with authority to take major decisions. The individuals should be allowed and encouraged to experiment and pilot a number of ideas. And most important of all, the management philosophy and ethos must recognise that failures are an inevitable part of the process which should be tolerated rather than punished.

MANAGEMENT TIP: Create a small eCommerce team reporting to a senior business director.

Do not leave the design and implementation of an eCommerce operation to the IT department. Many Internet offerings have been created that are technically sound but are not integrated with the rest of the business. Similarly, even when an Internet or eCommerce venture proves successful, speedy decision-making and significant investment is required to scale up the operation quickly. The only way to manage the development of an eCommerce operation within a large, and possibly bureaucratic, organisation is to delegate responsibility for its development to a small team with decision-making powers. Appointing a senior business director to oversee the development will provide the support and buy-in from other senior business executives.

Once you have started on an eCommerce initiative, either the venture will prove an instant success (unlikely) or it will disappoint (more probable). In the event that you have managed to find the right formula and the demand from your customers is overwhelming, you must be prepared to move pilot to large-scale implementation quickly. For example, Amazon's revenues in 1995 were less than $1 m. Revenues for Quarter 4 of 1996 were over $8 m and doubling every quarter. Achieving scale became critical to Amazon's success. Its revenues in 1996 were three times the figure of its nearest on-line competitor, strengthening its position in the market.

Large-scale implementation may also require heavy expenditure on marketing to secure a dominant share of the market. Companies must also be prepared to cannibalise existing products and services. In other words, senior managers must be prepared to 'eat their young' or lose the business.

> **MANAGEMENT TIP:** Slash costs in existing channels as you scale up your Internet presence.
>
> Many companies make the mistake of assuming that, because the average cost per transaction on the Internet is significantly lower than through traditional channels, a move into cyberspace will reduce overall costs. Not true. Unless companies are prepared to cut costs and investments in their existing delivery channels (close distributors and shops, redeploy or lay off staff, cancel capital investments), the overall cost base invariably increases. Don't fall into this trap.

There are major advantages from thinking big, moving fast and scaling quickly. Dell Computers has a tremendous 'first mover' advantage over its competitors. One of its biggest rivals, Compaq, waited until 1997 before it announced its own direct sales offering over the Internet. As a result, it has a lot of catching up to do.

9

Make a start

If you have read the briefing thus far and have concluded that you are ready to consider eCommerce in a serious way, there are four relatively straightforward steps to follow in order to get started:

- Step 1 – Conduct an honest self-evaluation of your capabilities.
- Step 2 – Decide if there is a business case for change.
- Step 3 – Gear up for implementation.
- Step 4 – Just do it!

Step 1 – Conduct an honest self-evaluation of your capabilities

The questionnaire on the following two pages provides an opportunity to assess how well your company scores in an evaluation of its eCommerce capabilities based on the guiding principles outlined in the previous chapter.

Like any questionnaire, the objectives of completing it are both to make you think through the issues as well as providing you with a benchmark score. You may want to interpret the scores as follows:

- If you score more than 70 out of 100, your company is well-positioned to achieve success on the Internet.
- If your score is less than 50, you are unlikely to be successful and you probably require a major rethink.
- Between 50 and 70 means that you still have considerable work to do to make the Internet work for you.

Step 2 – Decide if there is a business case for change

Business cases are designed primarily to help managers make investment decisions. Don't automatically assume that 'there is a business case – we just haven't written it down'. Prepare one, or insist on having it prepared for you. Use the template from Chapter 7 if you need guidance. Also feel free to have the business case checked out by somebody who has implemented an eCommerce initiative, if necessary.

Question	Possible Answers	Score
Do you have a strong 'customer proposition'?	We have a unique proposition, which has clear benefits to the customer and has already been successfully test-marketed.	20 points
	Our customer proposition is good, and we believe it will be received positively by customers when it is launched.	10 points
	Ours is essentially a 'me too' offering – but it seems to work for our competitors.	5 points
	Score out of 20 (insert your score here):	
Is senior management fully committed?	Senior management is committed to fundamental changes and our company has already appointed a senior executive to lead our eCommerce initiatives.	15 points
	Senior management understands eCommerce and appears to be prepared to make changes to make our eCommerce initiatives work.	8 points
	Senior management has an elementary understanding of eCommerce but our eCommerce initiatives are only being driven by one or two middle managers.	4 points
	Score out of 15 (insert your score here):	
Have you adapted your sales and distribution (or procurement) processes for 'cyberspace'?	With the help of our key customers, we have fundamentally redesigned our key processes and have carefully planned the implementation of these changes to ensure that our eCommerce offering will work effectively.	15 points
	We have agreed to make some changes to our key processes such as sales and distribution.	8 points
	Our existing processes are more or less the same as before. Although there may be some teething problems, we're sure we'll be able to work through the issues as they arise.	4 points
	Score out of 15 (insert your score here):	
Are you providing valuable 'content' for your customers?	Our Internet site is one of the most innovative in the industry and is updated constantly using a variety of in-house and externally commissioned 'content' material.	10 points
	We regularly update our site with new material although we have never considered going to external providers to improve the range and quality of our content.	5 points
	Our Internet site is well designed and easy to navigate. We provide information on our products and services and we even have a picture of our CEO on the site!	2 points
	Score out of 10 (insert your score here):	

Question	Possible Answers	Score
Are you using eCommerce to consolidate your suppliers and cut costs?	Since agreeing to introduce eCommerce for procurement, we have planned to halve the number of suppliers we deal with, and cut procurement costs through obtaining more favourable rates from our remaining suppliers.	10 points
	We will probably reduce the number of suppliers as a result of implementing eCommerce in our company.	5 points
	Our policy is to maintain a wide range of suppliers in order to maintain competition between them.	2 points
	Score out of 10 (insert your score here):	
Do your customers contribute to your eCommerce offering?	We have designed our offering with the help of our customers who have the flexibility to design and order their own products, while we have been able to reduce costs in our traditional distribution channels.	10 points
	Our customers can provide us with the feedback which we will use as an input into our design process.	5 points
	We have a good traditional Web site that is generating leads for us.	2 points
	Score out of 10 (insert your score here):	
Have you created links to other sites or alliances with other companies?	We have researched our offering in great detail and have created formal alliances with a number of other organisations. This generates a 'club' atmosphere among our customers and builds loyalty to our Internet site.	10 points
	We have started to create links with a number of organisations to make our eCommerce offering more attractive to customers.	5 points
	Our Web site should generate a reasonably high volume of traffic.	2 points
	Score out of 10 (insert your score here):	
Are you 'thinking big, starting small and scaling quickly'?	We have an ambitious end game, resources committed to a number of options and will invest heavily in successful ventures.	10 points
	We are ambitious but only investing in one option to achieve our objective.	5 points
	We are testing the water with an eCommerce venture and will see how it goes.	2 points
	Score out of 10 (insert your score here):	
	Overall score (out of a maximum of 100) is:	

Major investment decisions should be signed off by senior management, which often means getting it approved at board level. Make sure that the key decision-makers understand the basics of eCommerce and the Internet, including its strengths and limitations. If necessary, provide guidance in the form of one-on-one briefings or workshops to educate them. Similarly, if you are on the receiving end of a business case and are asked to approve it, make sure you are supplied with enough information to help you decide whether to accept it or not. Again, check back to Chapter 7 for guidance if necessary.

The world of eCommerce is ever-changing and difficult to predict. The chances are that the initial business case will need to be updated on a regular basis. Insist that this is done. Too often, the initial estimates of costs and benefits are inaccurate, and a recasting of the business case serves to refocus senior management attention, allowing them to scale up, adapt or kill the initiative as appropriate.

Step 3 – Gear up for implementation

Just as it is important to prepare a realistic business case, a pragmatic implementation plan will save you going back to the board to explain why the project has been delayed or why additional resources are needed if deadlines are to be kept. An important part of the implementation plan is an assessment of the capabilities of the organisation to implement the required changes.

Despite the hype, electronic commerce is a relatively new area. Few people have direct experience in thinking through the type of on-line service that is required, the interplay with other delivery channels or the change management skills required to make a successful implementation. Perhaps more important is the assessment of the management capability of the company to lead and drive through the necessary change to ensure your eCommerce initiative is a success. Assessing the technical competence of your organisation is another important issue. With the IT departments of many European companies tied up in preparation for Year 2000 and EMU, the use of external technology support may become a necessity.

Finally, don't be afraid to seek outside help if this is not your area of expertise. There are many external organisations that can provide assistance with everything from designing a Web page to re-engineering your processes and integrating your computer systems. Consultants may be expensive, but so are failed implementations.

Step 4 – Just do it!

Need we say more?